The Art of Black and White Photography

About the Book

Taking pictures in black and white has always been a popular form of expression in the field of photography. For the beginner, they are a way to add a bit of classical flair to their photos, in an attempt to make more of a visual impact. For the professional, they present an opportunity to work in a medium that is different, and which makes for quite an adventure in itself, editing wise.

While it may appear fairly simple to shoot in black and white, or monochrome, getting a result that actual titillates the mind and the imagination is quite complicated.

There are a myriad of factors to consider when going full monochrome. The image format and how much editing flexibility it provides, the amount of contrast, from pitch black to snow white, in the photo, the textures, the shapes and the depth, are just some of the factors. The range of techniques that go into monochrome photography make it an art form that needs to be learnt in depth, before exploring further possibilities.

Whether you are new to photography in general, or you haven't really explored the black and white realm, or even if you are experienced yet looking to do more in monochrome, this guide can benefit you to no end. Be it simply framing the photo, to advanced techniques such as editing monochromatic RAW, this guide has all the tips and tricks you need, to make an experience out of black and white photography.

Remember that you may not have access to all the accessories, equipment and/or software mentioned in the book. If so, you can always look for an alternative to any of the aforementioned, but which functions similarly.

Contents

Introduction

Black and white photography is considered by many as the most fundamental of genres. Technically there is some truth to this, seeing as the very first photos were black and white. What is less realized is the fact that black and white, despite being very simple and straightforward, is fairly complicated in essence.

If you look at pictures that are over a hundred years in age, you will notice that there is so much more to that simplicity, from a truly artistic point of view. The pictures appear as if to tell a story that begs to be heard beyond the visual surface. It looks surreal, mysterious and beautiful, all at once.

Some say that color is a form of visual distraction that distracts from the emotion, the expression and the meaning of the photo. They attribute the beauty of monochrome to the lack of such distractions. This is true to some extents. A photo that does not have much in the way of vibrancy is looked at more deeply, more intricately and differently. The human mind tends to look at the deeper meaning of the photo and understand the expression of it.

This unique perspective did not exist back when black and white was the only color scheme available.

In the olden days, the entire world saw itself on the screen in black and white. For many years this continued, till the first of the subsequent color-capable equipment was invented. After that, black and white saw a rapid decline in interest, with more and more people turning towards the vibrant new medium. However, here was one community who kept monochrome alive, and turned it into the art form that we view it as, today.

Photographers have long regarded black and white as the quintessentially artistic genre, the Shakespeare, Rumi and/or Bach of the craft. Based purely on the ability of a black and white picture to tell a story, this opinion does not seem too far off. If you master shooting in black and white, you do gain a much deeper understanding of the various nuances of photography.

The benefits of black and white don't end there. You gain a better sense of what contrast, highlights, shadows, textures and shapes can mean to a photo, and how to capture them better, be it in monochrome or full color. You learn what to look for while composing a photo. Tonal contrast, patterns and textural spreads are all mostly overlooked aspects of a photo. These aspects are not only paid attention to in monochrome, but they make the basis for the photo itself, making them come of the deciding factors behind how good a photo is.

The lighting of a photo is another very important aspect of the medium, one that is observed carefully in color but worked on religiously in black and white. Because of the absence of any distractions in the form of color, we tend to seek out the illuminations in the photo as visual focal points. This just adds to how much an apparently simple, colorless image contains within itself in way of detail.

The art of black and white photography is therefore, without a doubt, the finest of all photography techniques. This makes it paramount for any photographer to accumulate practical experience in the genre and practice black and white photography extensively. Not only will it make them more well-rounded artists, but it will provide them with more in-depth knowledge of photography as a whole.

Let us then look at the art and what it entails.

Visualization

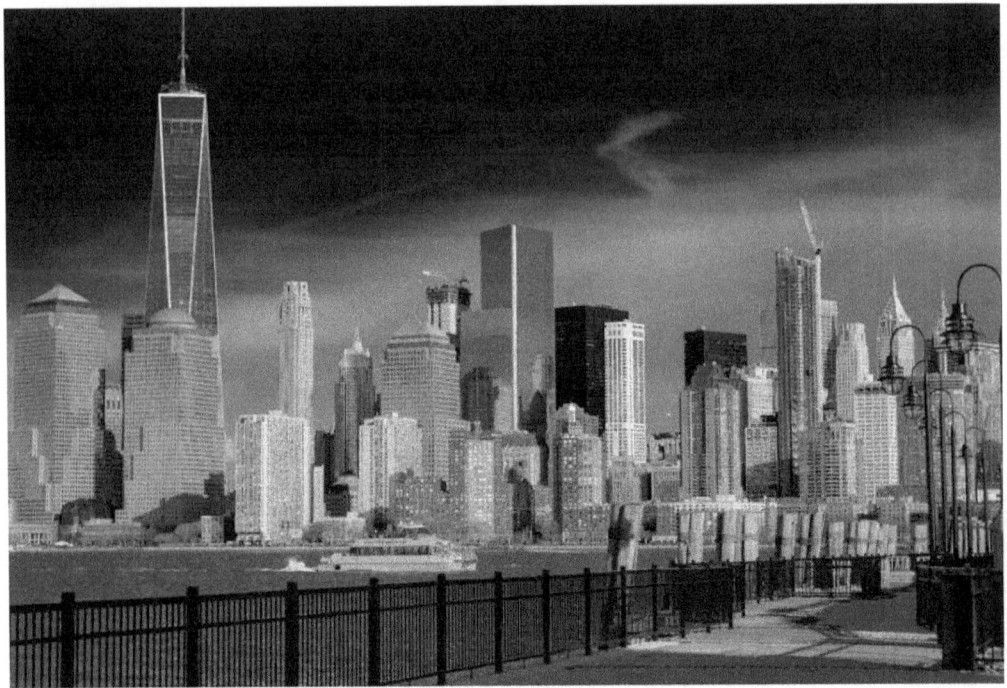

The ability to see the photo as it will turn out, before you have even taken it, is a rare one. Not every photographer can take one look at a scene through their eyes or even through the viewfinder, and know exactly how the image can potentially turn out. This sort of visualization comes after years and years of practice, as well as a natural creative sense.

In the world of black and white photography however, this ability is all the more important, and incidentally, even more rare. When you are shooting in monochrome, the picture may turn out colorless, but the same won't apply to the scene as you are looking at it through the camera's viewfinder or with your eyes in full color.

Some modern cameras, especially DSLRs, have an option that allows you to look at the scene in front of you on a screen, instead of through the viewfinder. When you set the camera to shoot in monochrome, the live view may be shown in monochrome as well. This does present a tremendous advantage in the visualization process. However, it does not instill, let alone develop, the ability to see past the colors in the scene through the naked eye, and visualize the scene in black and white.

Seeing in Black and White

Once again, it is important to reference the start of the art, when there was no other choice for the photographer to visualize the photo before releasing the shutter. Before digital photography was introduced, film was the medium that everyone used to work on. And since there is no way to preview a photo with a film camera, the photographer had to rely on their own visual ability and intuition. This also meant that they had to understand the optimal settings for every lighting and scenic condition.

What limited their ability to learn on the go also made them truly knowledgeable about the art. This is why the photographers of old and indeed the ones that have stuck to film were able to make their photos look as beautiful as they did.

The photographer of today does not have to learn about the intricacies of photography in such a way. They can simply click, preview and repeat, to eventually end up with something truly praiseworthy. However, if you truly wish to master monochrome, you will have to develop an eye that looks beyond all the distractions such as colors and vividness, and peer into the depths of the scene.

In order to do this, you can start by looking at a particular scene for several seconds or even up to a minute at a time, if it is a landscape or architecture. Look at all the subjects that stand out in the picture and learn where in the picture they will be located. After that, try to imagine all the color draining out from the picture. If you achieve this at the first try, you are already well on your way towards the next step.

Next, look at the colorless image with your mind's eye, and observe all the shapes, textures and tonal variations in the image. Your understanding of the tonal variations will ultimately decide how well you are visualizing the picture. If you can gauge where the black will blend into the white, you will know from what angle to frame the photo. If you can see how all the various shapes and textures emerge to the forefront in the black and white image, you will then be able to translate that into a superior monochrome photo.

How Monochrome Differs in Terms of Detail

Detail is something that exists in a photo regardless of whether it has any color or not. It is how the human eye sees it, where the difference lies. In general terms, the sharper the picture and the higher the resolution, the more detail there will be in the picture. But once you take away the distracting color, is when you really start to focus on the nuances of the image.

You immediately look for finer details in the absence of color. Your eye automatically goes for that condensed texture, that stark contrast in terms of tone, between 2 subjects, and the softness or hardness of the image overall. All of these details, which are already present in the photo, start to become clearer and more defined. And as you become more accustomed to black and white photography, you start paying attention to these details in all of your images, be they colored or monochrome.

Seeing more detail in grayscale is natural, seeing as when one major aspect of the photo, the color in this case, is absent, you will look for other things that are present and in this case, that is the detail in the image.

The other major reason for us seeing more detail in black and white is the vividness of certain subjects that may be in the colored image, which would distract from most of the finer details. For example, if you take a photo of a study room, with a bright red vase placed on a table, chances are that the person, who is looking at the image, will be immediately drawn to that vase. This is due to it being a color that instantly draws attention to itself. It is only later that you start to observe the other subjects in the image of the room.

Now, if that image were to be shot or converted into black and white, the distraction factor of the red vase would be nullified, and chances are that it might be the last thing you consider. This is because taking a picture that doesn't have any pronounced subjects in it creates an illusion of uniformity. It makes all the subjects look the same, differing only through tonal variation.

The amount of tonal variation that a particular photo has depends upon both the photographer's own preference as well as the lighting conditions present. Even considering the variables though; a black and white photo is likely to have more tonal variation than a colored photo, at least from a visual perspective.

It can be rightly said that a monochrome photo differs from a colored photo through the majority of the components. And it's these components that define a true, dynamic monochromatic image.

Understanding the Various Components of a Dynamic Monochrome Image

We learned previously that a monochrome image can vary across almost the entire range of photographic components. Now, while there is a lot that goes into a photo, components wise, there are some clear distinctions between grayscale and color, when it comes to what makes a photo.

Following are some of the components of the black and white medium that are particularly pronounced, in the medium. Please note that while the components explained below are generally what make a black and white photo unique and attractive; even inside the medium, there are quite a few variations, such as soft monochrome, dynamic monochrome, smoky, stark etc.

Clear Whites and Blacks

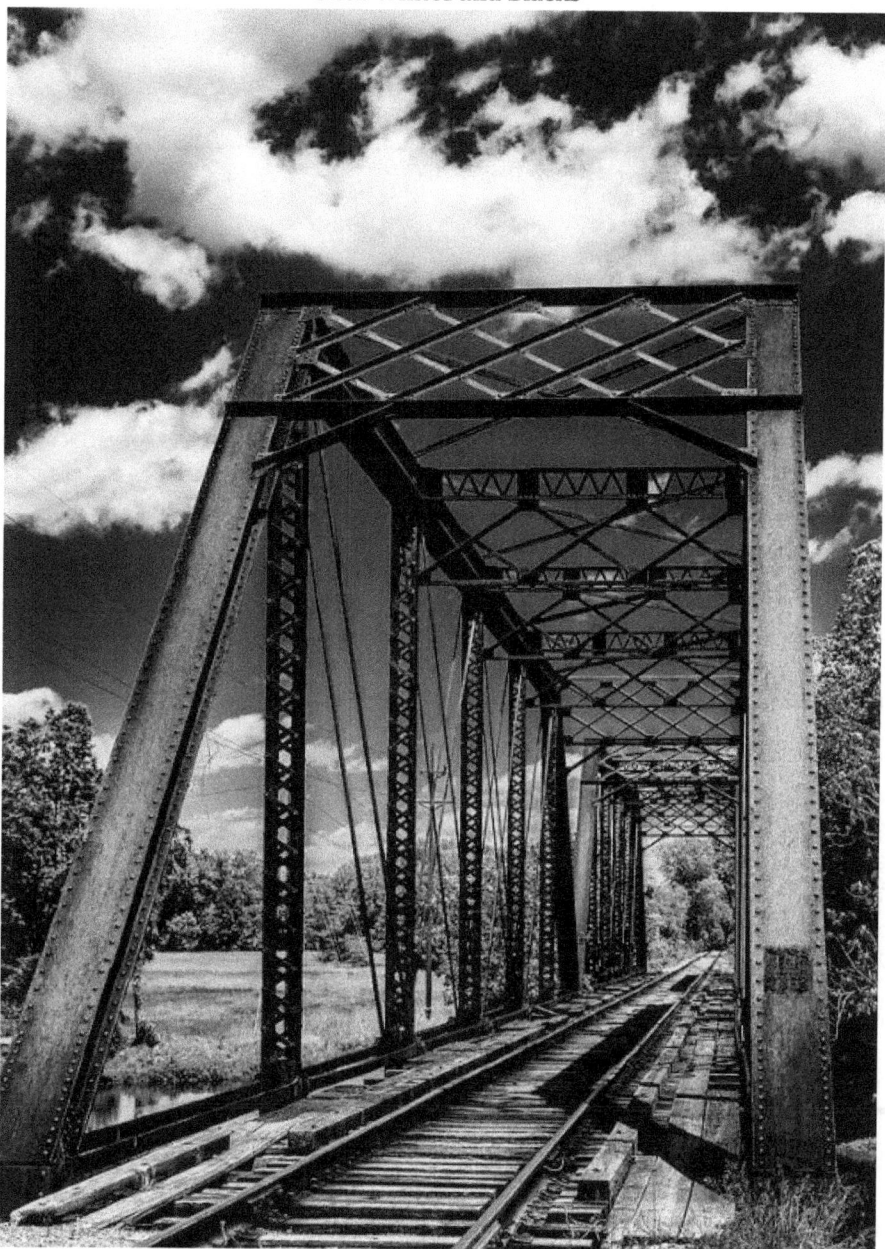

The first component is of course, a clear distinction between the blacks and whites in an image. Now, while gray is an integral part of the medium, hence the name grayscale, the clear black or clear white aspect of the image, however minor, is what makes black and white as amazing a medium as it is.

When you look at a black and white photo, the clear tones stand out the most, at first sight. This is the same effect that bright, lush colors such as red have in a colored image. In the case of a colored image, this effect is enhanced if the colored subject or object is juxtaposed against a background, foreground, or level field that is duller than itself. Taking that very same image, if we were to convert it into black and white, chances are that that object may not stand out to the viewer's attention as it did in color, losing that distinction to another object that is clearly black or clearly white.

In landscape photography, a standout object could be a brightly colored tree or a house in the middle of a valley. In black and white image, that house may not stand out as clearly as the surrounding mountains, if any, due to their snowy peaks. It is important to note that such landscapes are more often than not, taken in color. However, for the sake of understanding the component, you could try it out practically as well.

The impact of the photo due to clear blacks and whites is more visible in dynamic monochrome photos. These are images that have a stark contrast between dark and white. They have the most white or black space in them, with minimal tonal dilution to take away from the visual impact of the image. In such an image, the focal point has to be either completely black or completely white. This will enable the camera, if it is already on monochrome or grayscale mode, to highlight whichever tone you are focusing on, automatically creating a clear contrast between the two tones.

While excessive white space is seen as more artistic than aesthetic, you will need to have an ample amount of white space, in clear patches for more dramatic appeal.

Overexposure or Underexposure

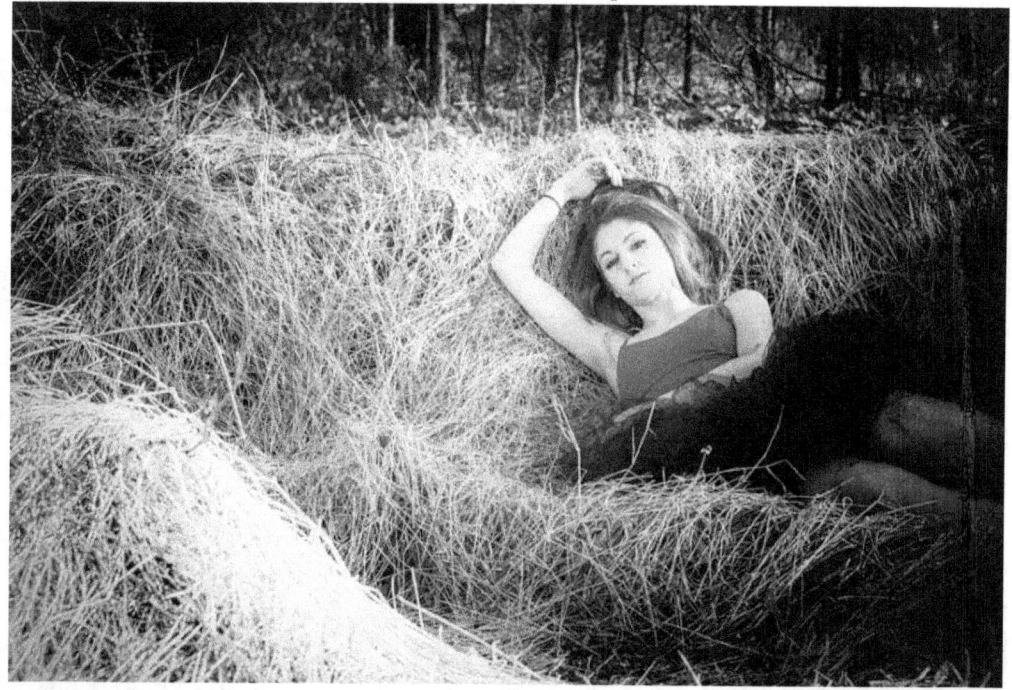

This component demonstrates the difference between the mediums very well. In colored photos, the exposure has to be exactly right, in order to maintain the integrity of the image, color depth wise. It is the exact opposite in a monochrome image, where colors are not present therefore not considered as a factor at all.

You may overexpose a black and white image, to bring out the whites in it. This will dilute the tones to an extent, depending on how much you have overexposed; to the point of graying out all the blacks. It will make for a very dynamically monochrome image, with a brightly energetic vibe to it. This is especially effective for action or movement shots in black and white, where the emphasis has to be on the energy of the subject.

Take note that while overexposing may make for a more dramatic shot; it tends to dull out several of the textures that could otherwise add to the mood and textural richness of the photo. This is why you should only overexpose images that do not contain a variety of different textures.

Underexposing will do the very opposite of the aforementioned exposure technique, sacrificing energy for texture and mood. If for example, you are taking a photo of a cloudy sky, you will want to bring out the mood of the photo which is contained within the cloudiness. This calls for rich textures and generally more detail to the photo, which underexposing the image will inevitably do.

When you underexpose an image, you essentially allow the shadow in the photo to become more visible. When these shadows are more pronounced, the whites in between them become highlighted and the grays become more sharply defined. This is what causes the sharp detail in the photo to emerge; utilizing more of the available pixels in the way of image fidelity.

Tonal Balance

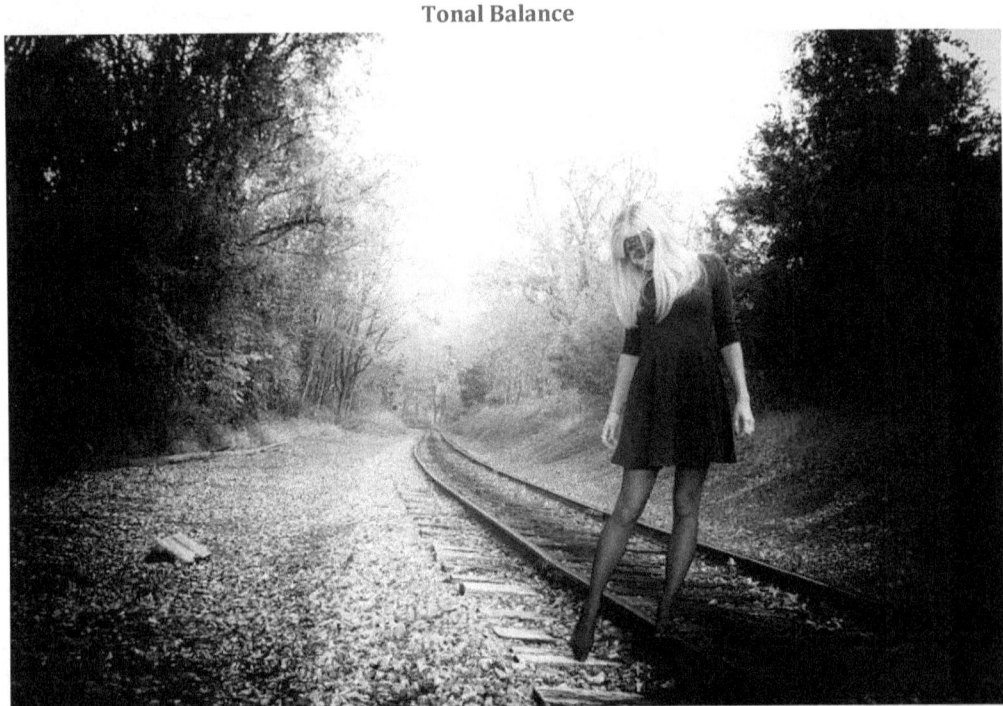

A good black and white image, especially a dynamic one, has an evenly balanced amount of black and white to it. This is because of the tonal balance which is necessary in an image, so as to not look unappealing and in some cases, overexposed.

For example, if you are taking a photo of a suspension bridge with a dual perspective, you will need both detail and contrast. The detail aspect pertains to the metal surfaces and the tarmac, while contrast is from the light shining in between the cables and arches etc. Taking this photo in broad daylight, with sufficient white space to make a frame of sorts, for the main subject which is the bridge, will make for a very balanced image. While the side surfaces of the bridge will show up as pitch black, the textures will be visible in the arches, due to the light reflecting off the tarmac and falling on to them.

It is important to note that not all pictures will be as balanced as is ideal. Some subjects such as those shot against a completely or mostly white backdrop will inevitably be more exposed than others. For such photos, you will need to make sure that the subject is sufficiently black, or in case of a person, that their clothing is dark enough to strike a balance.

Lines and Patterns

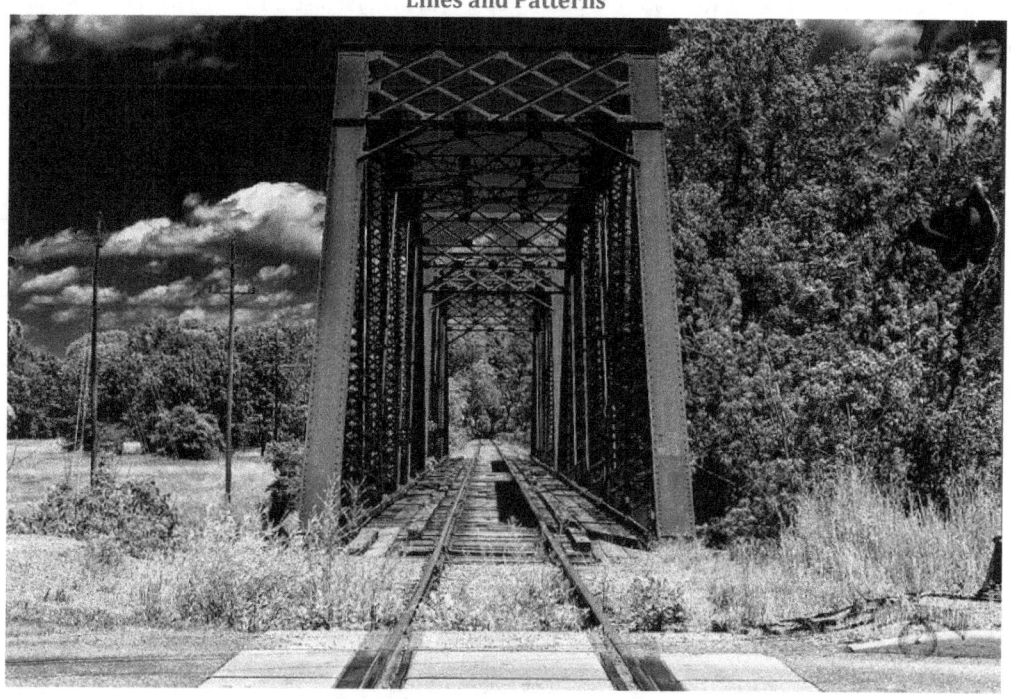

Patterns represent uniformity and certainty, in the ideals of fine art. The same is true for photography, especially monochrome photography. A pattern is q way to draw the eye of the viewer towards various points in the photo, creating a network of focal points. If the photo has a centerpiece, even if it is a part of the patterns, your eye will immediately be drawn to it, creating even more interest in a particular image.

Lines are more direct in their approach. They immediately take you to the point of focus, acting as directional arrows in a way. While they may be any manner of congested or convoluted, they are a sharp and direct, which makes the image more visually direct as well as detailed.

If an image has both features however, it will do both take the eye of the viewer on a visual journey through the picture, as well as present some very exciting framing and composition opportunities.

When framing an image that has lines as well as patterns, always try to look for a major focal point such as where the lines converge. A very good example of this is the dual perspective that we talked about earlier. Perspectives in general always lead to a focal point. Add in some patterns in the image for more of a dramatic effect.

Shooting a Variety of Subjects in Black and White

There are various other components in an image, both major and minor, that need to be taken into account, chief among which is what you are photographing in the first place. The subject is the central part of the photo and as such, deserves some thought and planning.

This is also the most variable component, as there are potentially limitless subjects, each with its own unique set of qualities.

Black and White Portraits

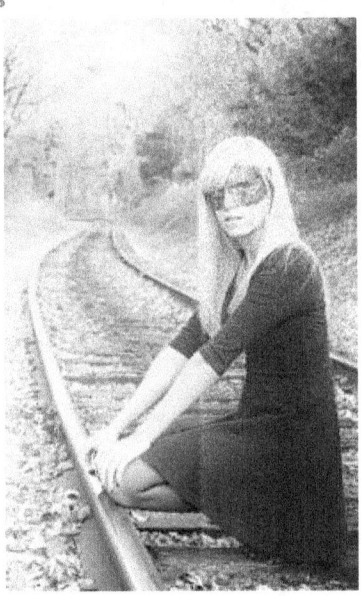

"If you want to shoot fashion, shoot in color, but if you want to shoot emotion, shoot in black and white." – Anonymous

Take portrait photography for instance. The subject is very clearly defined here, thus making it one of the simplest forms of photography. When shooting portraits in color, you will need to take the various tones and shades into account, in order to not make the skin of the subject look unevenly colored. The lighting angle, composition, and the expression of the subject, all have the potential to drastically alter the image itself.

When shooting portraits in black and white however, a lot of the variable factors go out the window. Skin tone is as important anymore as the exposure and the contrast can take care of that. Colors and hues don't have to be bothered with as they are not visible. When these factors are missing, the weight of the image falls on the lighting, contrast and composition.

Skin looks different in black and white. No matter how tanned or flushed a person's face is, the color won't show up in the photo, for which you will have to compensate with the lighting. You will have to shoot the face from an angle where you get the majority of the lighting directly on the face, with the light fallout starting from the temple and ending just behind the ears. This is the preferred technique for indoor, studio portraits, and it places that viewer's focus directly on to the subject's face, especially their eyes in a black and white shot.

For shooting portraits outdoors, focus on the eyes. Use the spot metering option and focus directly on the eyes. If you have the camera itself set on black and white mode, you will notice in the preview that the eyes will be the most detailed aspect of the entire image. This is because the absence of color directs the eye straight towards the centerpiece of the image, the person's eyes. Not only will this add drama in the shot, but it will result in an extremely detailed image that is full of emotion.

Black and White Landscapes

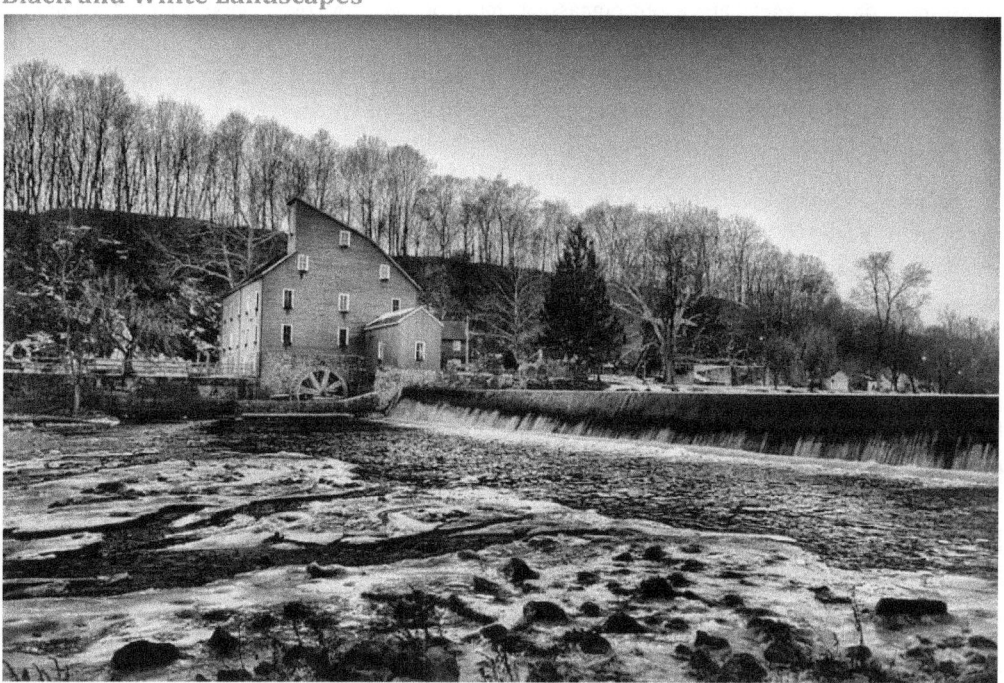

Portraits are generally easier to understand and shot in black and white. This is because the subject is directly in front of you and you have the freedom to play with the shot as much as you like. Landscapes are different in the way that they have a lot of room for artistic error. This means that there is a lot that could go wrong, when shooting a landscape in black and white, resulting in a less than appealing photo of an otherwise beautiful scene.

When you shoot anything, a landscape in particular, in monochrome, you are basically taking the essence of whatever is in your viewfinder, and capturing it in the form of a photograph. O do this successfully, you have to make sure that you are getting as much of the essence as possible. This makes shooting in RAW an absolute necessity.

Next, try to find or compose a view that has the most texture in it. The texture could come in any form or shape. For example, if you are shooting a sweeping valley, it will be better to have a group of trees or a mostly forested patch, in the image, ideally with a mountainous frame. This will add more detail to the image, which the grayscale mode will automatically draw.

The foreground and the background are both equally important in monochrome landscapes. This is because of the smaller aperture that you will be shooting on. Landscapes are generally never shot at an aperture value less than f/16, with f/22 being the ideal aperture setting, at least for daylight shots. For low light or night shots, you will obviously need a slower shutter speed. The bulb setting will be ideal as a learning tool, due to its ability to teach the user better shutter control.

Landscape photos in general are 'all-encompassing', meaning that they cover a large area and feature a lot in one photo. This is why you should try to get as much dramatic detail in one shot as possible. Try to balance out the image by composing in such a way that there is a balanced amount of black and white in the picture, with the rest being filled by various shades of gray. This means that you will more often than not, be underexposing the image, and making any minor adjustments later, through editing.

An additional advantage is the ability in more recent DSLR cameras, to display the image in monochrome on the LCD screen. This feature is called Picture Control in Nikon Cameras, and Picture Style in Canon systems. This way you will have a lot more control over the image, through the ability to make adjustments to the photo before you have even clicked.

What to Look For in a Subject

There are many photographers, some extremely famous, who have made black and white photography not just their preferred medium, but their preferred method of expression. People like Peter Lindbergh, Ansel Adams, Herb Ritts and Henri Cartier-Bresson, all are famous for their magical monochrome expressions. The majority of them, with the exception of Adams and Bresson, shot fashion predominantly. Still, the emotion and the stories that they capture in each shot are truly remarkable.

This is mainly due to the mastery over the craft that the people have. The ability to tell a story is necessary if you are indulging in black and white photography, and every subject in the medium has to be visually worthy of telling that story.

From the technical aspect, that means the subjects you choose to shoot need to have all the qualities that make a good scene into a great photo. The qualities include the aforementioned balance between the blacks and whites with sharp contrast and softer grays, some fine textural details, tonal variation, ideally some lines and patterns, and artistic appeal.

In case of grayscale portraiture, look for a subject with the most facial detail, or an ability to express deeply and powerfully. Professional models are naturally adept at expressing emotionally, sometimes through the eyes alone. Alternately, you could photograph someone who hasn't posed in front of the camera at all. In landscapes, you should look for an area with lots of textures and detail, ideally some clean lines and patterns as well.

Choosing a subject is one of the most subjective aspects of photography. While this is true for all photographic mediums, the absence of color and as a result of that, the outpouring of drama and emotion in monochrome makes it very important to choose a subject that will appeal to anyone who sees the image.

Tones

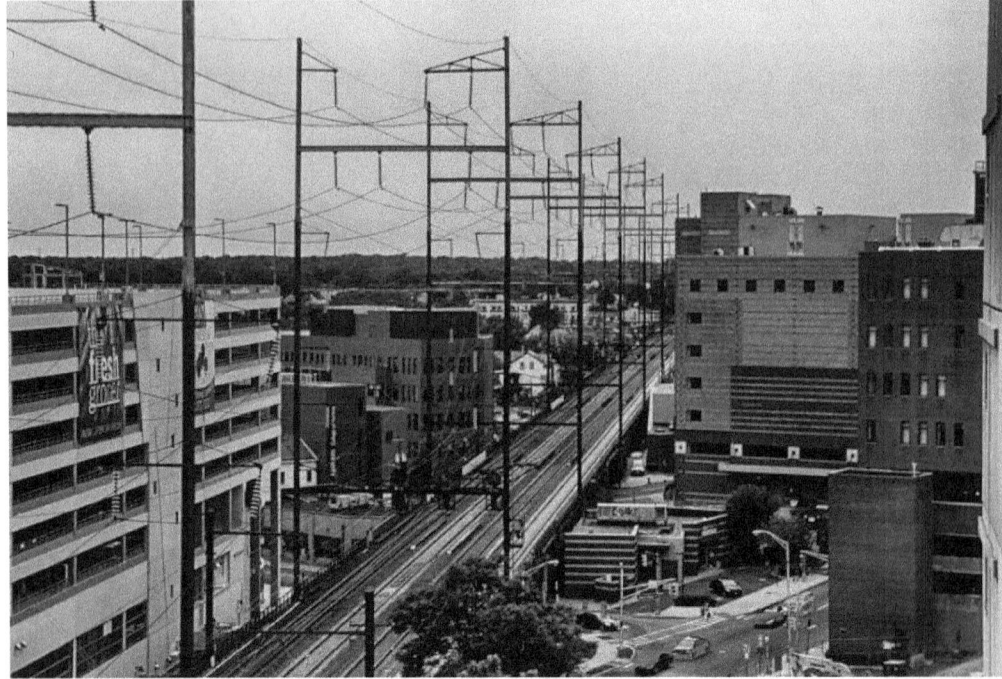

Black and white are polar opposites as tones. Even in color photography, they are the exact opposites of each other, and are added to induce more of a dramatic feel in the photos. In black and white photography, they are once again the opposites; only this time they are all that your eye will see. There are however, other parts of the image that are very important in grayscale imagery; the grays.

Grays have several purposes in monochrome, chief among which is the role of a subtle bridge between the sharp contrasts. The amount of gray in an image can differ, with the least being added in dynamic monochrome, and the most in portraits and softer landscapes, such as those involving fog or misty areas.

A very popular technique in monochrome photography is to capture a broad range of tones, with multiple shades of gray in between. This serves to soften the image a bit, the ideal scenario for a gentler image that is not meant to be very striking. Shooting portraits, especially small children, is the ideal practice with a wide tonal range.

For softer tones, you can either shoot in places with a natural haze or fog, or artificially induce some, whether in person or through editing.

The best black and white photos, by and large, are the ones that exploit the tonal differences the most. While each photographer has their own preference as to how they like their black and white photography, it is important to explore and find out for yourself, how you like to express.

As always, it is very important to shoot in RAW, as black and white photos have the most room for editing. This is because of the fact that even though they are expressions unto themselves, they are somewhat blank canvases as well. As far as tones go, you can always increase of decrease the dark or light tones present in the image via editing software. You can also add mist, as mentioned, for a considerably softer image with a smoky finish.

Details and Textures

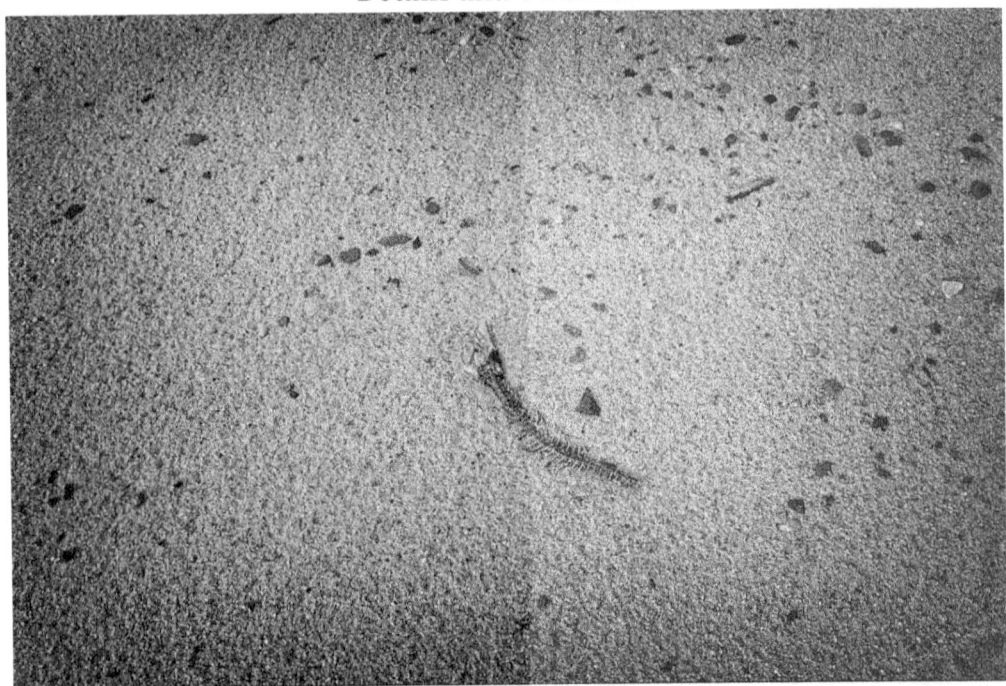

As mentioned earlier in the book, textures are a very important part of grayscale, seeing as they emerge to the forefront when there is no color present to take away the eye of the viewer from them. Also important to note that while soft and smoky monochrome images are attractive in their own way, they lack significantly in one of the foremost aspects of black and white photography, namely textures and details.

The general rule of thumb here is that the less the image is exposed, the more the fine textures and details will reveal themselves. You may even be surprised at how many intricate textural details you can bring out in a particular picture, by simply converting it into black and white, or shooting in black and white in the first place. While this is simply a lacking on the part of the human eye to see fine textures when the photo is in color, it can also be attributed to some of the textural blending that is often done when lush colors are employed.

Texture and detail, while different in a way, are somewhat connected in black and white photography. When we talk about texture, we are in fact talking about the amount of detail that appears in our images. That detail, in the form of texture, could be anything, from the freckles on a person's face to jagged rocks and boulders on a cliff side, to a carpet of trees in a deep valley. As long as there is an ample amount of textures, it will produce a very powerful effect, especially when coupled with low exposure.

Contrast

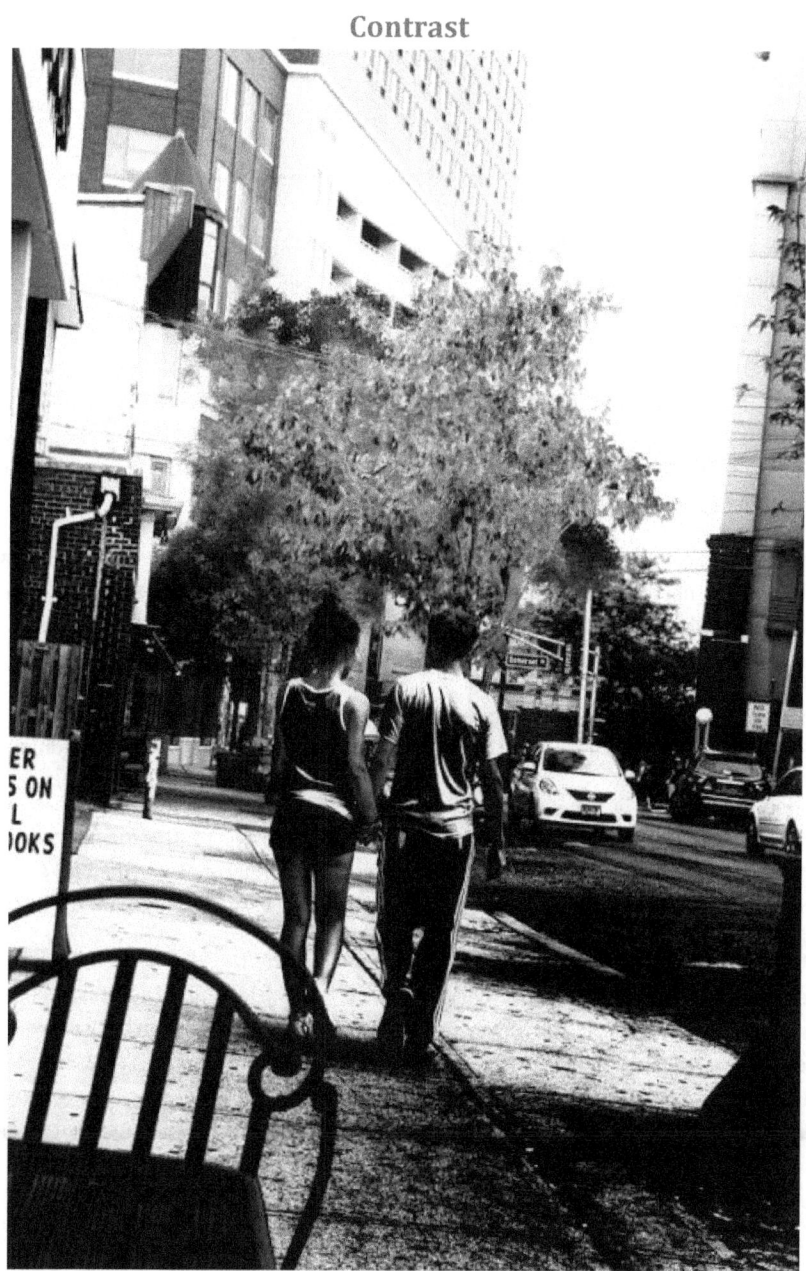

Contrast can be considered the defining feature of a black and white image. So much so, that if you look at it, the entire medium is based on the principle of contrast, both visually and theoretically. The simple distinction between 2 colors makes the basis for every monochrome image as well as the medium itself, which is why you need to put effort into understanding contrast and how it can be implemented into an image, especially a black and white one.

The interesting thing about contrast in black and white photography is that the 2 shades involved in it, namely black and white, tend to complement each other when both are shot in high contrast. This means that if you have a darker background behind a lighter subject, the subject will visually 'pop out' more. Similarly, if you have a light background and/or surroundings behind a dark object, the object will be more clearly visible. In the latter scenario however, while there will be greater contrast around the darker object, the detail on the subject itself will reduce in clarity.

The reason for the loss of detail is that when you juxtapose black against white, the eye tends to be 'blinded' by the brightness of the background and/or the surrounding. This is the exact phenomenon we call snow blindness, when the snow that we see becomes so bright, due to the sunlight falling upon it that it blinds the human eye, making even otherwise clearly visible objects difficult to see.

The truth is that the detail is there, it is simply harder to see. Which is why you have to be careful to not add an excessive amount of contrast, whether it is natural (due to sunlight) or through editing software.

If you are shooting a subject or a model in black and white, one very creative technique is to have portions of your image sharply contrasted, with other portions displaying softer tones altogether. This can be done in a fashion-esque style, with the model dressed in softer tones and the background or the surroundings sharply contrasted, and vice versa. This adds a bit of visual balance with the photo as well as combines multiple aspects of the black and white medium.

You can also use the camera's own exposure settings to control the amount of contrast your photos have. If the scene you are capturing already has clear and defined blacks and whites, set the exposure to the level corresponding to the shade that you want to be more pronounced. This means that if you want to highlight the lighter shades, you should overexpose the image slightly, taking care not to overdo it, which would then result in the loss of detail. And if you want to show the darker tones more clearly, underexpose the image slightly, taking care not to turn the whites into grays.

Shades of Gray

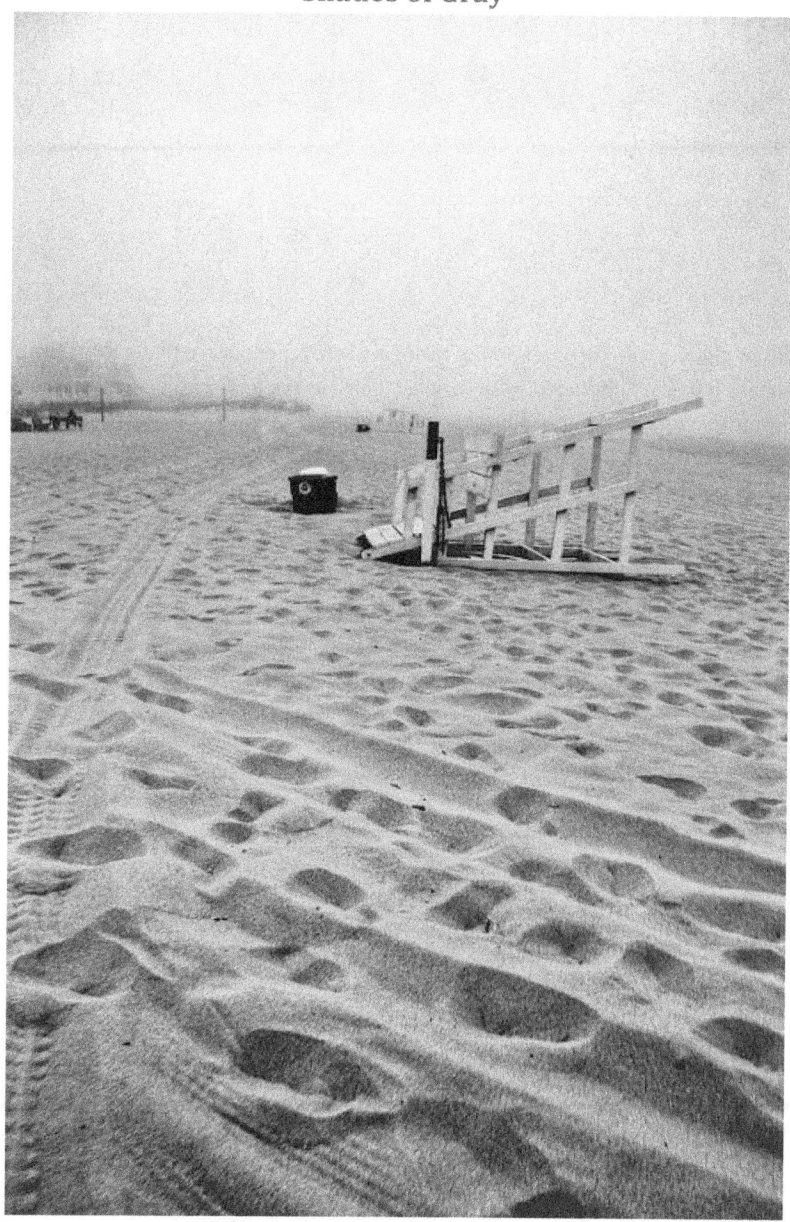

Gray and the various shades of it can be seen as the life blood of monochrome photography. While whites and blacks form the body of the work, gray is the element that bonds the other 2 together. This is the reason why black and white photography is also called grayscale, as it is the bulk of the monochrome tonal range, with pure black and white being the ends of said range.

When you look at a scene with the intention of taking a photo, chances are that a lot of the elements within the scene will be medium toned, with very few being at the ends of the aforementioned tonal range, Now, when you take the photo in black and white, these medium tones are what will show up as gray, with the darker tones being black or white. What you will notice here is that even if there was a multitude of colors in the scene, the end result will simply be various shades of gray.

Gray itself is a combination of black and white, as colors. In fact, if you look at the technical aspect of it, black and white are simply the darkest and lightest shades of gray, respectively. The rules of dynamic monochrome dictate that you show these two shades in the majority of the composition, with the middle shades occupying minimal frame space. This can bring about a very dramatic and active photographic result, but it tends to take away from the character off the image, to an extent.

Gray is used to give the photos a bit of a softer feel, while at the same time adding a touch of mystery and character to them. This can be done by shooting at the standard exposure, with care taken as to not include many sharply black or white tones in the image. Shades of gray can be found in abundance in nature itself, as well as almost any scene that you come across.

If you photograph moving or falling water, in the evening, with a longer shutter, chances are that it will show up as gray, with minimal texture. Similarly, if you shoot mist and fog, it will show up as gray as well. Both these phenomena are due to the lack of texture and detail in both photos, which created a blurry effect in the photo.

Editing Black and White

Having learned what black and white photography entails, and how you can improve yours, let us take a look at what can be done after the pictures have been shot, to improve them even further.

Common Editing Software for Black and White

Editing black and white images can be done on any photo editing software. Some of them have more features and options than others, which makes them more suited to this kind of function.

Following is a list of some of the software. Know that you may have to purchase some of the filters and extra options that the software offers and the editing job requires. It is also important to note that black and white photos are best shot and edited in RAW, using Adobe Camera Raw. This retains a lot of the details in the photo, allowing for a greater range of modifications that can then be done. However, if you wish to avoid the complications and all the intricate details that come with RAW imagery, it is best to use Photoshop and the ilk, for your monochrome photos.

Silver Efex Pro

This is one of the most beautiful and simple software that you can use to edit monochrome photos. It is basically a plug-in from the Nik collection that can be accessed and used on a variety of editing software such as Lightroom and Photoshop.

What makes this plug-in stand out from the rest is the number of presets that are provided to the user. You can then utilize those presets as individual starting points, in order to gain a better understanding of how the various modification elements work.

As mentioned earlier, texture and detail are integral to the medium. While both Lightroom and Photoshop have options for the enhancement of texture, Silver Efex Pro has more of said options, making it superior to both the base software in this aspect.

Contrast can be modified across a much more diverse range as well, as compared to the base software. You can also amplify the whites and blacks in the photo, as well as increase the amount of contrast in the photo, while retaining some of the original softness of the image.

All in all, Silver Efex Pro makes it a lot simpler while increasing the possibilities for editing.

Adobe Camera Raw

When you are shooting in Raw, the best editing tool that you can have in your suite is Adobe Camera RAW. This software is perhaps the most versatile and detailed in this aspect, with a vast array of editing options on offer to the editor.

Unlike the previous software, which is exclusively used for monochrome images, Adobe Camera RAW is more versatile, with many of the options dedicated to colored images. Even then, you will be hard pressed to find better RAW editing software.

Adobe Photoshop (CC, Elements)

The master of all editing software, Adobe Photoshop and its versions are aimed towards photographers of all skill levels, with the single biggest collection of editing options. Elements is better for the amateur photographer, with more direct and photographer-centric features.

Editing Features

Following are some of the most effective editing features that can be used on black and white images.

Dodge and Burn

This tool can be used to enhance or tone down the shadows and the highlights in the black and white image, similar to what the photographers of old used to do in dark rooms. This is a method to increase the contrast in the photo, while adding some detail in areas where it is otherwise hidden. The textures are also enhanced with this tool, with more visible sharpness in the photo where the tool has been applied.

Levels

The Levels tool can also be utilized to alter the contrast to your liking in the monochrome image. If the image has more blocky portions of black and white, or crisscrossing lines of white over black and vice versa, you can use the selective editing feature that you get with the Levels tool.

Curves

Functioning in a similar way, the Curves tool is used to make adjustments to specific areas of the photo, which is extremely useful in bringing out the detail in the areas that you want to sharpen, while the rest of the image remains comparatively softer. The best part about the Curves tool is that you can do a lot more precise alteration, with it, as compared to the Levels tool. This is especially useful if you want to implement the change on to certain areas of the image.

Conclusion

While black and white photography is a medium with its own rules and regulations, it is important to know that like every other genre of photography, it is best to play around and experiment as much as you can. This will not only polish your skills and enhance your artistic intellect, but it will open an entire world of photographic possibilities for you to experience.

About the Author

Ryan Crane is a well-known name in international published photography. Ryan developed his photography skills through painstakingly long hours of research and trial and error. Having carved a niche in the world, he now aims to help others who are just starting to step into the world of photographic art. Visit ryancranephotography.com to start learning today! Click improveyourphotographyonline.com, if you are a photographer looking to improve their craft.